LIFE SKILLS

Written by Keilly Swift

Illustrated by James Gibbs

Up, up, and away!

As you set off on your life's adventures, there will be high points, low points, and all the points in between. This book is designed to help you navigate your journey. Get to know yourself, believe in what you can do, build confidence to tackle challenges, and grab some exciting opportunities along the way.

Reilly Swift

Penguin Random House

Author Keilly Swift

Editor Katie Lawrence
Project Art Editor Lucy Sims
Additional editorial Abi Luscombe
US Editor Jane Perlmutter
US Senior Editor Shannon Beatty
Production Editor Dragana Puvacic
Senior Production Controller
Edward Kneafsey
Jacket Coordinator Issy Walsh
Jacket Designer Elle Ward
Managing Editor Jonathan Melmoth
Managing Art Editor
Diane Peyton Jones
Creative Director Helen Senior
Publishing Director Sarah Larter

Illustrator James Gibbs
Educational Consultant
Wynne Kinder, M. Ed.

First American Edition, 2021
Published in the United States by DK Publishing
1450 Broadway, Suite 801, New York, NY 10018

For the curious
www.dk.com

Contents

This book is packed full of helpful tips.

What are life skills?

Imagine having your own toolbox that you can use to handle whatever life might throw at you. That's exactly what life skills are. Developing life skills will help you solve existing problems, and step into the future full of confidence and ready to tackle all kinds of challenging situations.

This tower includes the five areas of life skills in this book.

The best thing about life skills is that no matter where you're starting from, you can keep on building...

Finding solutions

In **Chapter 1**, find out how to make good decisions and solve problems, both big and small.

Ways of thinking

Learn how to approach issues from different angles, think outside the box, and gather information to form your own opinions in **Chapter 2**.

Communicating

Whether it's talking, listening, or the way you can speak without words, **Chapter 3** is all about building the valuable skill of communication.

Understanding feelings

Consider all the things that make you unique and try putting yourself in someone else's shoes to figure out how they may be feeling in **Chapter 4**.

Coping skills

From small, day-to-day challenges to more stressful situations packed with strong emotions, you'll find a lot of coping strategies in **Chapter 5**.

Finding

If you've ever faced a tricky decision to make or a problem to solve, you know how tough it can be. Learning different ways to break things down and work through options can help you make confident choices and find the best solutions.

Things might not work out exactly as you'd like every time, but learning from your mistakes is one of the most valuable lessons in life.

solutions

Making decisions...

Making decisions and solving problems are important skills that often go together. As you read this book, you'll learn tips and tricks that will help you develop these skills.

Decision time
Take time to make decisions—but not too much time. It's easy to rush into things too quickly, but not making your mind up can also be a problem.

Everyday choices
You make little decisions every day, from what shirt to wear to what to have for breakfast. Many choices don't need much thought at all, which means you can save your brainpower for bigger decisions!

Options and outcomes
Think about your different options and what their outcomes might be. Writing things down can be helpful, especially for a complicated decision.

Looking back
After you've made a decision, take time to think about how things turned out. Remember, everyone can make the wrong choice, it's part of learning.

Not this again!

It's a fact of life that sometimes you think you've solved a problem, but it comes back again! The same solution might not always work a second time, so try to think about what has changed. Can you look at things in a different way?

Ask questions

To come up with solutions, it can help to ask yourself a lot of open-ended questions, such as: "What would be my ideal outcome?" or "Who might be able to give me advice?"

Remember the goal

Problem solving is about finding the right ways to deal with an issue. In order to solve a problem, you might need to make decisions along the way. It's important to keep your goal in mind, since it's possible to make decisions but never actually solve the problem!

Piecing together

There are often many steps you need to take to solve a problem. For example, if you're always running late in the morning, the steps you might take could be to lay out your clothes the night before, and set your alarm for a time that's a little bit earlier.

...and solving problems

Mind map

A mind map is a way of breaking down your options when making a decision. It shows the different choices you could make and what might happen, so you can organize your thoughts.

Spend it all.

Should I spend or save my allowance?

Spend some, save some.

Save it all.

Map key

- Decision
- Options
- Pros
- Cons

Try making your own mind map and following the roads to help you make a decision.

I can have a nice treat right now!

I won't have any money left at all.

I can have a small treat now and some money to save.

It will take me longer to save for something I really want.

It won't take that long to save for a bigger treat and I'll have money saved if I need it.

I won't be able to buy anything right now.

Draw your own

This is a very simple version of a mind map. When you draw your own, you can use many pros and cons to help you make a decision.

Listen to yourself

It's said that intuition is your connection to your subconscious—the area of your mind that can influence you without you being aware of it. Taking some quiet time can help you tune in to what that part of your mind is telling you.

Trust your feelings

Sometimes we reject our own feelings, maybe because they are different from how everyone else is feeling. Your inner guide, however, is often right, so trust your feelings and explore the answers your intuition is trying to give you.

Following your inner guide can lead to making better decisions.

I've got a feeling

One of the most powerful tools you can use when you're faced with a tricky situation is your intuition. It's sometimes called your "gut feeling," and it can help you make decisions and solve problems.

What is intuition?

Your intuition is a strong feeling you have about something without thinking too hard about it. There are times when you just know something is right or wrong. Paying attention to this feeling can help you know your own mind. Here are some tips to help develop your powers of intuition.

Pay attention

Your subconscious picks up on more than you might think. Paying attention to what's going on around you means that you're gathering lots of little clues and bits of information, which all feed into your intuition to help you make the best decision.

Can you think of a time when your intuition has helped you? It may be that without knowing why, you just knew where to find something that was lost!

Sleep on it

There is a reason people say that they will "sleep on a decision." While you sleep, your subconscious runs through all the information that you've picked up and tries to make sense of it. After a good night's sleep, you may find that you wake up with the perfect solution to something that's been bugging you!

Write in a journal

Making notes about any issues you want to tackle and any thoughts you have about things is important. No matter how random these ideas may seem, writing them down can help you see things more clearly, and figure out how you are really feeling.

Use your intuition to help you piece together issues you're facing.

Put everything together

There are times that using your intuition can be really valuable, and other times when you need to think more and weigh your options. Often, you'll find these two skills work hand in hand as you face different situations and difficult decisions.

Taking your time

Everyone makes **wrong choices** sometimes. Taking some time to **think about** why things didn't **go as you planned** is a valuable skill.

Stopping to think

Maybe you made the **wrong choice** because you didn't **stop to think**, or you just went along with **everyone else**.

Learning

Sometimes, you **can't avoid** making the mistake, but did you **learn** something for **next time**?

The mistake maze

No one likes making mistakes, but everyone makes them sometimes! It can be tricky to find your way through mistakes, but learning from them can be even more useful than getting things right the first time.

Saying sorry
Sometimes you might do or say something you **regret** because you feel **angry**. Saying **sorry** is a sign of **strength** not weakness.

Having honesty
Being **honest** and having the **confidence** to say "I know I made a mistake" **shows a lot of character.**

Reaching your goal
If you've made **mistakes** along the way, when you reach your **goal** it feels **extra special!**

Finding a way through after making a mistake shows that you can handle almost anything.

Process it

Dealing with your problems can be tricky, and sometimes you won't know how to solve them. One of the best ways to tackle a problem is by breaking it down. Here's a process that can help.

The marbles aren't making it to the end of the marble run!

What's the problem?

Start by figuring out what exactly the problem is. Try to sum it up in one sentence if you can. Then write another sentence about what you would like to happen instead.

What are the causes?

Now think about what could be causing the problem. It could be one thing or several things. Are the causes linked or separate from each other?

Brainstorm possible solutions

Try to think up ways to solve the problem. They won't all be perfect solutions, so carefully consider the pros and cons of each option.

Make a plan

Write down what steps you are going to take, what you might need, and who you might need to ask for help.

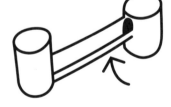

Action stations

Now it's time to put your plan into action. If things aren't going as you hoped, don't be afraid to go back a step and change your plan.

There's the problem! I hope this works.

Review outcomes

Whatever the outcome, whether the problem was solved or not, it's important to take time to think about how things went. It's all part of the learning experience!

Problem-solving machine

Look how this wacky machine takes a real-life problem and puts it through the problem-solving process to come up with a solution that works.

> I'm not getting along with my little sister. I'd like to find a way to help us get along better.

The causes

We're not interested in the same things.

She can be annoying.

My sister wants to hang around with me all the time.

Brainstorming

Brainstorm ways to solve your problem.

Possible solutions

Try to be more understanding and find ways to keep calm.

Set aside some time for you to do things together.

Only suggest doing things that you're interested in.

Tell her to leave you alone.

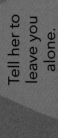

The plan

Think carefully about whether your solutions would work or not. These options might upset your little sister.

Some solutions might not work, but that's part of the problem-solving process.

Every Tuesday, take turns choosing to do something to do together.

Talk it out with your family and see what they suggest.

Review in three weeks

Tuesdays aren't working because we are too busy. Let's try Sunday afternoons instead.

Now that we also have a family meeting once a week, we get to talk about any problems. It's going well!

Did the plan work?

I'm getting along much better with my sister. We still argue sometimes, but now I have more ways of dealing with it. We are spending a lot of time together, but I can also do things by myself without upsetting her.

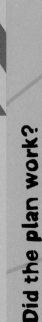

Try putting a problem you have through the machine to figure out what causes it. Come up with some possible solutions and a plan!

Small
steps

Some problems are so big they seem to be out of your control. But there are often ways to make things more manageable by taking small steps in the right direction. Here's an example:

> A big problem that worries me is that a lot of cats and dogs end up in animal shelters, but what can I do?

Think about the causes

There are a lot of different reasons why an animal ends up in a shelter:

- It may have been lost, and didn't have a microchip.

- Its owner may be sick, and can't take care of their pet anymore.

- The animal may have been abandoned.

These things are all out of your control, but are there still things you could do to help?

Pet sitting

You could ask if friends or neighbors need help taking care of their pets when they are away or sick. Before you do, be sure to ask a grown-up if that's OK.

Helping with appeals

Animal shelters sometimes put out appeals for things like old blankets and bedding. You could donate these things to make the animals' lives more comfortable.

What big issues do you wish you could solve? Are there small steps you could take to help?

Volunteering

Some shelters allow older children to volunteer with them. When you're old enough, you could sign up for this. It might even lead to a future career!

Fundraising

Raising funds for animal shelters helps them give the best care to the animals. Could you have a bake sale, wash cars, or raffle some of your old toys to raise money?

Fostering opportunities

Some animal shelters look for people to foster cats and dogs, to give them love and care before a permanent home can be found. Could you do this?

Responsible pet ownership

If your family adopts a pet, you should make sure you fully research its needs, so you know you can give it a happy and healthy life.

Ways of

Some people find it easy to come up with creative new ideas, while others are great at thinking things through step-by-step. You can develop both types of thinking.

In this chapter, you'll learn how to find a better way to get a task done, discover how to ask the right questions, and spot when information might not be quite right. It's time to get thinking…

thinking

Give it some thought

Creative thinking and critical thinking are skills that can help you in all kinds of situations throughout your life. Both types of thinking can help you make good decisions and solve problems.

Creative thinking

Thinking creatively means looking at something in a **new way**. It could be coming up with a **different** method, or **inventing** something entirely from scratch. Learning to think creatively means keeping your **mind open** so you consider all **possibilities**, being **flexible** in how you approach things, and sometimes **taking a chance** on trying something new!

Critical thinking

Thinking critically is a way of **processing information**. It means finding out the **facts** and **evaluating** things. Learning to look at things **differently** and **understanding** other points of view helps you see what's going on and form your own **carefully considered** opinions. Having this skill gives you the confidence to **decide** how you feel about something.

The pages in this chapter help you strengthen both your creative and critical thinking skills.

The power of wondering

One of the most powerful things you can do to think creatively is to wonder. Wondering means asking yourself questions, and opening up new possibilities. Here are some questions to get you started:

When you think something is impossible, just ask yourself "**What if** I changed something to make this work?" or "**What if** there's another way to do this?"

If you think a chore is taking too long, try asking "**What if** there is a way to do this quickly, but still do it right?" This could help you come up with a plan.

Wondering fun

Wondering can be just for fun, too. Let your imagination run wild as you think about these questions.

What if...

...trees could talk? What would they say?

...computers didn't exist? What would life be like?

If there's a particular food you don't like, ask yourself "**What if** I'd like it prepared in another way?" Whether it's in a smoothie or a stew, you could be in for a delicious surprise.

When you see something interesting, such as a painting or building, ask "**What if** there's a cool story behind this?" You could then do some research to see how close you are to the truth.

When you're writing something, ask "**What if** there is another way to say this?" or "**What if** there is a better word I could use?" This could help make your writing really original.

...I could build a robot using things I can find at home?

Can you come up with some more things to wonder about? Have fun discussing your ideas with your friends and family!

Getting creative

Exploring your artistic talents is a wonderful way to process your thoughts and feelings, or even spark creative thinking.

Creative expression

Here are some of the things you can do to express yourself creatively. Whatever you choose, being creative helps you see things from a different perspective.

Getting artistic

When inspiration strikes, try digging out your camera, paints, and pens. You may be inspired by a beautiful scene, or want to explore a subject you're interested in.

Photos and art can prompt all kinds of feelings and memories. You'll be creating something that can be treasured forever.

Think about what it is that makes something special to you and feel how you can bring that to life in your art.

Writing it down

Putting your thoughts and ideas down on paper is a great method to express yourself. There are so many types of writing you can try. You could plan what you're going to write, or just see where your imagination takes you.

Writing in a journal about things that have happened can help you make sense of them.

Coming up with a story or crafting a poem lets you explore your own thoughts and ideas.

Making music

Music can help you express loads of different feelings. Learning to play an instrument can help your brain work in new ways. It's no surprise that one of the greatest scientists of all time, Albert Einstein, played the violin!

Don't forget that your own voice can be an instrument, too. Whether it's singing or beatboxing, your voice is a powerful tool.

Listening to a lot of different kinds of music can help you figure out what instrument you might be interested in playing.

Putting on a performance

Taking part in the performing arts, such as dance and drama, allows you to explore your feelings and show them physically. It can also boost your confidence and self-esteem.

You could do ballet or hip-hop, put on a mime show, or learn a play based on your favorite book.

Whatever form your performance takes, remember that you're bringing something to the stage that no one else can—YOU!

Thinking creatively

Creative thinking is a skill that can be strengthened with practice, and is sometimes called "thinking outside the box." Here are some tips and tricks to help you get started.

Get inspired

Make a display or keep a book of everything you see that inspires you, whether it's a beautiful painting, a funny animal photo, or a cool gadget. One creative thought can spark another, and you never know what exciting ideas you could end up with to solve problems.

Can you think of something sillier than this dog's umbrella hat?

Be silly!

When trying to come up with a new idea that no one else would try, start by brainstorming the silliest things you can think of. Write down absolutely everything, no matter how ridiculous it sounds. Then come back to your list and see if it's the start of something great after all.

Put a llama on display.

Challenge what you know

There are many things you do without thinking. Maybe it's your morning routine, or the way you put your clothes away. Think! Could there be a better, or easier way of doing things? The smallest changes are sometimes the most effective.

What would Megan Rapinoe do?

Roll up clothes instead of folding them.

Think like someone else

Think about what someone you admire might do. It could be your sports hero, a celebrity you like, or someone in your life whose views you respect. Think about the type of ideas they might come up with to solve a problem.

Real-life examples

A sticky situation (1974)

When Arthur Fry's bookmark kept falling out of his book, he came up with the idea to use a type of glue to hold it in place. Post-it® Notes were born!

Successful failure (1970)

Apollo 13 crew: James Lovell, John Swigert, and Fred Haise

The Apollo 13 spaceship was almost at the moon when an oxygen tank exploded. The three astronauts on board had to move to another part of the spaceship, but it started to fill with dangerous levels of carbon-dioxide gas. The astronauts survived by creating a makeshift gas absorber from the items they had on board!

The situation

Imagine you're looking through a magazine and you spot an article about a new gadget. Before you decide to buy it, it can help to ask yourself questions about the article to make sure the gadget is worth it.

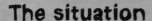

What?

The first thing you should ask is "What does this article tell me about the gadget?" This will help you figure out if the article gives a balanced review of the gadget or not.

Digging deeper

A great way to train your brain to think critically is to ask the right kinds of questions. Here's an example of when asking a lot of questions could help you dig a bit deeper.

Who?

Next, you might ask "Who wrote the article?" Was it written by someone who works for the manufacturer? Some people will write articles just to get you to buy their products, so it is important to research who the author is.

Think about other situations when asking these questions would be helpful.

I know just what I'm going to do!

OUT

When?
It is important to ask "When would I use this?" to help see if it's worth buying. You could also ask "When should I buy it?" Could you wait until your birthday, or for it to go on sale?

How?
When you've done all of your research, it's great to ask "How has my opinion changed?" Do you still think buying the gadget is the right decision?

Why?
You should ask yourself "Why do I need this gadget?" You might find that there is a similar gadget that you'd like better, or that there is something else that you want more.

Where?
Another question to ask is "Where could I get more information about this?" You might know someone who already has the gadget and could tell you more about it, or an adult could look up some reviews online.

You've been put in charge of creating some new rules for your school or a club. Follow these steps to come up with a plan.

Do your research

Now it's time to look into things a bit more. Talking to people is a big part of that. You could speak to the adults who made the rules or ask your friends for their ideas. It's good to talk to a range of people who think differently from you.

Can you tell me why you think that?

Question the information

Start by asking yourself a lot of questions. What do you know about the rules that are already in place? Why are the rules there? Who benefits from them? How would you like rules to change, and why?

Critical thinking cap

Putting on your critical thinking cap can help you carefully consider things and come up with new ideas. Here's how to get thinking critically about something.

Look at the big picture

Once you've gathered a lot of facts and opinions, you need to weigh up everything. Think about what is and isn't possible, and why people suggested certain things. Consider your own opinions, too.

New rules to consider:
- Ice cream every day
- Early finish on Friday
- Everyone to help with a gardening project

Test out some ideas

If you're unsure what effect something might have, you could test it out for a short time. By trying it out, you can see what works and get feedback from people about it. You might end up keeping the rule, changing it a bit, or scrapping it completely.

New rule for today only!

You need to help at least one person with something.

RULES

Put your plan in place

Now it's time to put your plan in place. If something doesn't work out as you hoped, you can always put your critical-thinking cap back on to review how it went.

You can use your critical thinking cap in all kinds of situations.

37

Pet News
Cat and mouse are best friends!

Daily Life
UFOs spotted over city

Tech Online
The robots are coming!

Stopping to think

It can be easy to think that what you see and read is always true. Here are some examples of when critical thinking can help you stop and question what's real.

I can't believe our favorite band was voted off the show. It must be rigged!

Yeah, they were the best! No way they'd be voted off.

What a scam! EVERYONE I know voted for them to stay.

Before you go online, you should always check with a parent or guardian. Remember that to use most social media sites you need to be at least 13 years old.

This cross between a giraffe and a hippo has been spotted on the African savannah.

Easy to think

These headlines are amazing. They are in a newspaper, so they must be true.

Stop and think

Could the headlines be exaggerated to encourage people to buy the paper? Ask an adult to help you research whether headlines are likely to be true in this type of newspaper, and to help you better understand the facts.

Easy to think

That band would never have been voted off. The show must be rigged, everyone says so.

Stop and think

How do you know the show is rigged? You don't know any facts yet, all you've heard is other people's opinions. Could you find out more about how the voting works?

Easy to think

What an amazing creature. I need to share this photo with everyone I know.

Stop and think

Wait a minute! Does this look too strange to be real? Ask an adult to help you research if this animal truly exists. Not all photos are real!

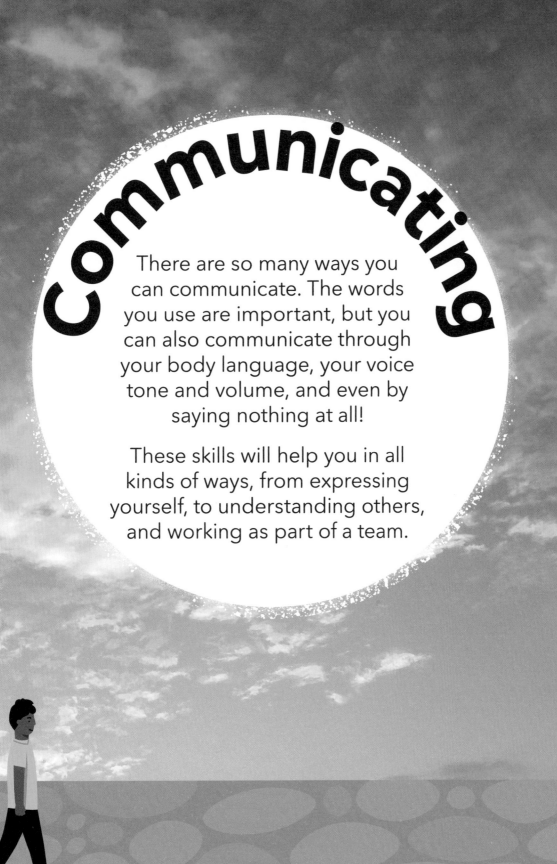

Communicating

There are so many ways you can communicate. The words you use are important, but you can also communicate through your body language, your voice tone and volume, and even by saying nothing at all!

These skills will help you in all kinds of ways, from expressing yourself, to understanding others, and working as part of a team.

The communication

Explore your communication skills with these challenges. Play with your friends, and have fun communicating things in different and new ways!

Topic cards

First you will need to pick the topic you're going to communicate. Here are some ideas...

- A movie you love
- A hobby you have
- An animal you like
- Your favorite holiday
- A meal you don't like

Once you have decided on your topic, you can choose one of these four challenge cards.

Miming

Can you act out your topic in 30 seconds without using words—just actions?

- What actions would communicate your topic in the best way?

- Remember you can use facial expressions, gestures, and even props to help you.

- It can help to exaggerate your actions, so that your friends don't miss anything

Challenge cards

Each challenge card asks you to communicate your topic in a different way. After you pick a card, your friends can guess what you're trying to tell them.

game

Think about other topics you might want to try communicating to others in this game.

Drawing

Try drawing a picture that sums up your topic. You have one minute—go!

- You can make your drawing as simple or as complicated as you like.

- Be as accurate as possible, and use a photo as a reference if you need to.

- You could add details, such as a face with an expression, or a thumbs up or thumbs down to show your friends how you feel about the topic.

Writing

Can you write a short paragraph to explain your topic? Try to finish writing in 3 minutes.

- Are you writing to tell someone more about the topic, or to tell them why you chose it?

- Make sure you include all of the important information about the topic.

- Have fun with the words. Could you include a rhyme or a play on words?

Talking

Without saying the name of the topic, can you talk about it for 30 seconds?

- Think about the best words you could use to really get your message across.

- Remember to stick to the topic. Try not to talk about something else.

- Avoid pausing or saying "um"— it's harder than it sounds!

Learning to listen

Learning to listen well is just as important as learning to talk. These top tips will help you take ideas in rather than just hear the words.

Wait for a pause

If there's something you don't understand or need someone to repeat, you should speak up. But don't interrupt anyone midsentence—wait for a natural pause.

5

Block out distractions

It's easy to get distracted by things, such as a TV that's on in the background. It's important, however, to keep your attention on what's being said, or you might miss something.

3

Make eye contact

Listening to someone can start with your eyes. Looking them in the eye shows that you are focused on what they're saying and that they have your full attention.

1

2

Listen with your whole body

It can help you listen if you make sure you're not fidgeting, fiddling with something in your hands, or tapping your feet.

4

Keep your mind open

While someone's talking, try not to jump to conclusions in your mind. It's best to wait to hear the whole story before you form any sort of opinion.

Feel it

Empathy means understanding someone else's feelings. If you share someone's sadness when they're telling you something sad, or their excitement at some good news, you are understanding things from their point of view.

Concentrate

If you start trying to think about how you're going to reply, you may find that you tuned out what someone is saying. Concentrate on listening, it's fine to take some time when it's your turn to reply.

Test your skills: Ask an adult to give you directions to somewhere in your neighborhood. Listen carefully and see if you can figure out where the directions would take you!

9

7

8

Picture it

Forming a picture in your mind of what you're being told can help you remember the key details.

6

Keep to the topic

Try not to say things that would take the conversation in a different direction. You can always wait until the end of the conversation and then mention something else that has interested you.

10

Show it

Show you understand what someone is telling you by mirroring what they say. It could be saying something like "That's amazing!" or even just nodding your head to show you're following what they're telling you.

Happiness

Shoulders back

Big smile

Chin up

Arms relaxed

When you're feeling nervous, using confident body language can help!

Anger

Red face

Clenched jaw

Arms crossed

Mirror work

Look in a mirror and see if you can show these feelings without saying anything! There are a few pointers here, but do whatever feels natural.

More than words

It's not just words that tell people how you're feeling. Body language can give away more clues than you think. Being aware of your body language and noticing other people's are very useful skills.

46

Boredom

Drumming fingers

Holding head in hands

Looking away

Nervousness

Wringing hands

Looking down

Tapping foot

Body talk

Body language can be very powerful. If someone rolls their eyes at you it can be just as hurtful as saying something mean. If someone is sad, a hug can show you care more than you could say with words.

Giving the wrong impression

Sometimes we form habits that can mean our body language is sending a message to other people that we don't intend to send. Here are some common things people sometimes do without thinking:

Scowling

It could just be because you're concentrating, but it may look like anger.

Biting nails

This common habit can be a sign of worry or stress, or it can just make it look that way!

Slouching

Maybe you're a bit tired, but sit up straight if you want to be alert and listen well.

Kennedy vs. Nixon

In 1960, a US presidential election debate was shown on TV for the first time. To most people watching, the newcomer, John F. Kennedy, was the clear winner since he looked confident. Those listening on the radio thought the more experienced Richard Nixon had triumphed. They, however, hadn't been able to see how much Nixon was sweating, which made him appear nervous.

Kennedy went on to win the election.

Studying the science

We communicate far more with body language than we do with words. Studying this nonverbal communication, called **kinesics**, can tell us a lot. For example, when two people are getting along well they often mirror each other's body language without realizing it.

It's how you say it

Adjusting the volume and tone in your voice can change the meaning behind your words. It's useful to think about not just what you say, but also how you say it.

Very loud
You should be very loud when you need to get attention immediately, such as in an emergency!

Volume
Using your voice at the right volume can help in different situations. It can affect how clear your words are and even reveal how you feel. You might speak quietly if you're feeling sad, or very loudly if you're angry.

Loud
It helps to speak in a loud, clear voice when talking to a group of people.

Medium
This is your normal volume, for everyday conversations.

Quiet
This voice is used when you don't want to disturb other people.

Very quiet
Sometimes you will need to whisper, like when your baby sister is sleeping!

Silent
When listening to someone, it's best not to use your voice at all.

Tone

Your tone of voice works with your volume.
The same words can have different meanings
when they're said in different ways.

Attitude

Sometimes a grumpy attitude can come across in your tone of voice, even when you use single words, such as "yes," or "no." Try saying these words in a mean way, then try with an enthusiastic tone to hear the difference.

Emotion

Your emotions can come across in your voice, just like your attitude. It's important to show your emotions in your tone of voice to let people know how you feel. Try saying "I'm going to school" in both a happy and sad voice.

Questions and statements

When you ask a question, your voice gets higher at the end. A sentence said without a higher pitch, at the end, however, is a statement. Try saying "You love music" as a question and a statement.

Speed

You might talk too quickly, especially if you're nervous, and people could find it hard to keep up—but, speaking too slowly might lose their attention. Try explaining something at a few different speeds.

Emphasis

Changing the word you emphasize, or draw attention to, in a sentence can completely change the meaning behind it. Try saying "I love ice cream," but emphasize different words each time and see how different it can sound.

Press record!

It can help to record yourself saying different sentences using different volumes and tones, to hear how they come across.

If you can't read someone's tone of voice, and are confused about what they are trying to say, then ask them.

What a team!

Teams work best when people communicate well. Have you been part of a team like the ones shown here? What did you notice?

Sports team

This relay team **works together** so they all know what their role is on the track. Before each race, they have to **communicate** with each other to make sure the team is working well. Most importantly, they have to **trust** and **stand by each other** even if they end up losing a race.

Fort building

These kids had a great time building their fort. They made a **plan together** and decided what job each person would do, such as gathering the things needed so others could build the fort. When **everyone has a role**, they can all feel proud of their **achievement**.

These runners need to communicate when they pass the baton.

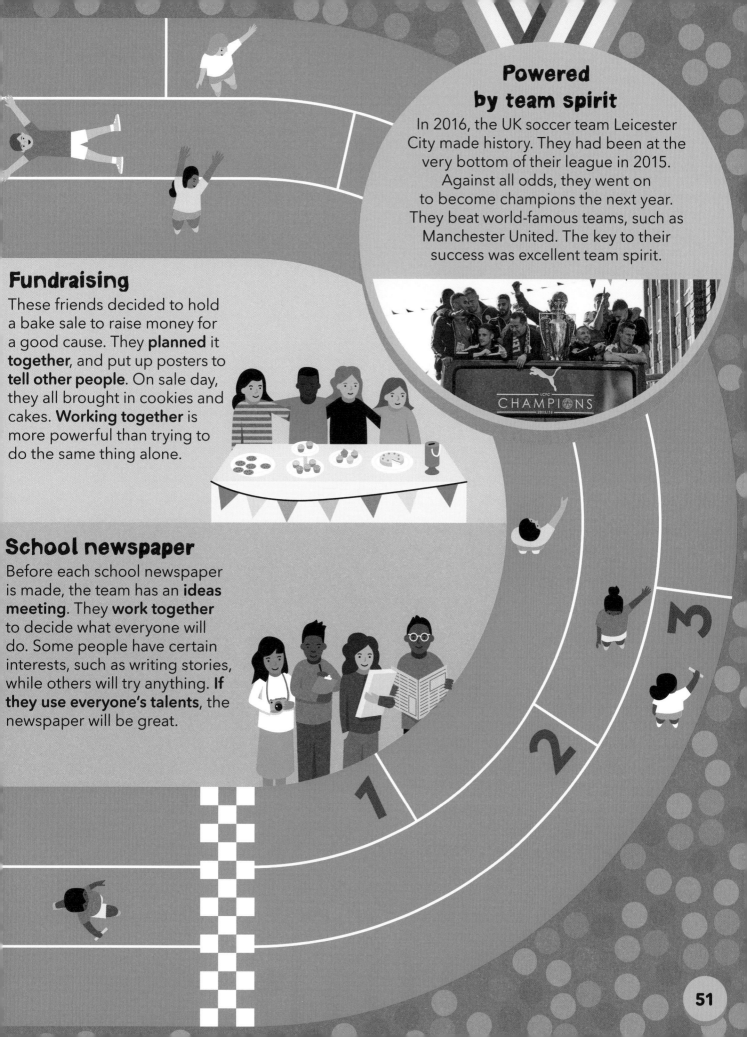

Powered by team spirit

In 2016, the UK soccer team Leicester City made history. They had been at the very bottom of their league in 2015. Against all odds, they went on to become champions the next year. They beat world-famous teams, such as Manchester United. The key to their success was excellent team spirit.

Fundraising

These friends decided to hold a bake sale to raise money for a good cause. They **planned** it **together**, and put up posters to **tell other people**. On sale day, they all brought in cookies and cakes. **Working together** is more powerful than trying to do the same thing alone.

School newspaper

Before each school newspaper is made, the team has an **ideas meeting**. They **work together** to decide what everyone will do. Some people have certain interests, such as writing stories, while others will try anything. **If they use everyone's talents**, the newspaper will be great.

Choosing the right words

When you're faced with a tricky situation, finding the right words can make a big difference.

disagree

no

talk

yes

sorry

listen

Asking for help

If you're struggling with a piece of homework, you may feel like giving up because you can't do it by yourself. Instead, remember that everyone needs help sometimes. Think about who may be the best person to ask, whether it's a teacher, a classmate, or a sibling. Here are some useful tips:

○ Tell them what you've tried so far. It may also help to explain how you are feeling.

○ If you're worried that they may not have the time to help you right now, then ask them when would be better.

○ Don't forget to thank the person who has helped you. Knowing they're appreciated will mean a lot.

There will be times when you disagree with someone about something that matters to you. You should speak up about how you feel, but not in a way that could cause hurt feelings. Here are some things that could help:

- First, you need to hear them out. Listen to the reasons behind their view and try not to interrupt.

- Then, when it's your turn to talk, show them that you have listened by using a phrase, such as "I understand what you're saying, but I think…"

- If they try to interrupt you or talk over you, it can help to say "I can see you feel strongly about that, but please could you listen to my thoughts."

"Don't be afraid to ask for help when you need it. I do that every day. Asking for help isn't a sign of weakness, it's a sign of strength. It shows you have the courage to admit when you don't know something, and to learn something new."

Barack Obama, former US president

Learning to say no

Saying no in the right way is an important skill to have. It's easy to say yes to things to make people happy, but sometimes you have to say no. Here's how you can do it in a positive way:

- It's important to be clear and to the point, so there is no confusion.

- You don't always have to justify your reasons, but it can help to explain. For example, "I don't want to do that because it doesn't feel right."

- If you're turning down an invitation, say it nicely and apologize if necessary. For example, "I'm sorry, I really wish I could come, but I have plans that day."

help

agree

Your mission

Imagine you're the leader of a team of superheroes, and decide what your mission is. Follow these steps to communicate and complete your mission! You could write your mission down as a story, draw it as a cartoon, or even act it out.

Express your feelings

Discuss which part of the mission is worrying you. Is there a problem that needs to be fixed?

Ask for support

Think about what you ma[y] need help with on the mission. What skills do other people have that could be useful?

Listen to others

Listen to what other people have to say, and take their comments into consideration.

Explain the goal

Sum up what your mission is. You may want to include some drawings or diagrams to help.

Communication superpowers

Feel confident

Strike a superhero pose! What are your skills? Use your confidence to help the team and believe in yourself.

Complete the mission

Be open to new suggestions and if the plan changes, don't forget to communicate that to others. Then, celebrate your success!

Say thank you

Thank anyone who helped you along the way and let them know how much you appreciate them.

Feel proud

Give yourself a big pat on the back for everything you've achieved. Finish the sentence "I am really proud of myself for..."

Communication skills are like superpowers. They are useful in all kinds of situations, such as starting a new group project. Practicing how you communicate can help when it comes to the real thing.

Understanding feelings

Have you ever stopped to think about all the things that make you, well, you? There's your personality, the experiences you've had, the things you enjoy, and so much more.

Considering the way you think and feel each day allows you to get to know yourself better, and can help you begin to understand how others might be feeling.

A capsule of you

In order to understand your feelings, you must first understand yourself. Making a time capsule is a great way to do this. Capture all of the things that make you uniquely YOU!

Inspiration

Here are some ideas for what to put inside your time capsule—but be as creative as you like. Seal your things inside a small box, a cardboard tube, o[r] a large envelope. Write the date on the front, and put it away to find again in the future.

A description of you by a friend

Seeing how someone else describes you and comparing it to how you see yourself can be really interesting. Is it similar or are there differences?

Treasured memories

What have you done that you think you'll remember forever? You could add some photos or old tickets.

Words or phrases

How would you describe yourself? Choose three words or phrases that you think fit best.

brave

artist

loyal

Self-portrait

Draw or paint a portrait of yourself. It doesn't have to be the greatest work of art, but try to add details that really capture you.

You could try making a time capsule every year to see how you've changed!

A special talent

What talents do you have? It could be playing a sport or an instrument, or even whistling tunes! Add them to your capsule.

Playing the violin, age 10

Hopes for the future

Whether they're grand plans for a future career or places you'd like to visit, make sure you capture your ideas. Try including pictures from newspapers and magazines.

Things I'd like to do

Are there things you'd like to practice over the next year? Write down how you'd like to work on them. It will be fascinating to look back and see how far you've come.

Favorite things to do

What do you like to do for fun or to relax? Write these down on paper, or add photos and drawings to your time capsule.

Personality quiz

Just for fun, here's a quiz to help you get to know yourself a little better. Try it out on your friends and family, too!

1 Which phrase describes you best?

A. A really thoughtful person
B. A very funny person
C. A supercalm person
D. A person who takes the lead

2 Which creature do you think you're most like?

A. A unicorn
B. A colorful peacock
C. A relaxed cat
D. A playful dog

3 If you had a free afternoon, how would you spend it?

A. Writing a story
B. At a theme park
C. Chilling out at home
D. Playing sports

How to play

Make a note of the letter you choose for each question. When you're done, count up how many of each letter you have.

Mostly As

You're a creative and thoughtful person, who can sometimes be shy. You are often lost in thought, and can easily entertain yourself because your mind is full of wonderful ideas.

Mostly Bs

You love being around people and having fun. You're happy being the center of attention, and you like to keep people entertained. You like to try out new things.

4. What type of movie would you choose to watch?

A. A movie that makes me think
B. A comedy
C. Anything relaxing
D. An adventure movie

5. Which of these things would stress you out the most?

A. Being too busy to think
B. Not being able to see my friends
C. Having a disagreement with someone
D. Being stuck inside on a sunny day

6. Which of these future careers would you choose?

A. An author or painter
B. An actor
C. A yoga instructor
D. A firefighter

7. What would you like to do with a friend?

A. Make or bake something
B. Play any type of game
C. Listen to music
D. Go to the park

8. What would you want to do on vacation?

A. Read a book in the shade
B. Make new friends in a pool
C. Relax in a hammock
D. Explore the area

9. What color best fits your personality?

A. Deep blue
B. Vibrant yellow
C. Calming green
D. Bright red

10. How do you like to let your feelings out?

A. Writing in a journal
B. Talking with friends
C. Meditating or walking in nature
D. Going for a long run

Mostly Cs

You are a very calm and patient person who likes to keep the peace. You prefer to be in a relaxed environment. You are usually very composed, and you don't get flustered easily.

Mostly Ds

You love getting outside and staying active. You like being a leader, and you work hard to get things done. If someone is in trouble, you're the first to offer help.

Everyone has a mix of traits, and your personality is not set in stone!

Future feelings

Noticing how you feel in situations means you may be able to figure out when you'll feel that way again. For example, if you know that something may make you nervous, you may make you to deal with that feeling before it happens.

Think back on the day

Just before you go to bed, think about the different emotions you felt during the day. Set aside ten minutes, and consider the reasons for your feelings and how you reacted to them.

I had a long walk in the park so I feel really relaxed and tired.

I had a great day out with my family, so I'm feeling happy.

I felt disappointed because I failed a test today. I didn't want to talk about it.

relaxed

miserable

curious

unhappy

bored

frustrated

delighted

annoyed

shy

angry

ecstatic

sad

scared

down

excited

happy

nervous

Taking a moment

Processing your feelings means taking time to think about your emotions. It helps you to stop bottling things up, and to realize how you really feel.

Sharing and caring

Sharing how you feel with others can help you process things. It can also mean a lot to people if you check in with them. Just asking someone how they're feeling can be really powerful. The strongest friendships are built on caring about each other's feelings.

I was nervous about performing in a show and I had butterflies in my stomach.

I was furious when my brother borrowed my new T-shirt without asking.

lucky

disappointed

over it

proud

embarrassed

worried

content

tense

confident

thankful

tired

Today I felt...

Keeping a journal, or diary, can be a great way to relieve stress. It can also help you develop a deeper understanding of your feelings and the things that are important to you.

Using your journal

Remember, nobody else will see your journal so use it in a way that works for you. Here are some tips that might help.

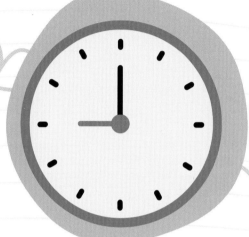

It can be helpful to get into the habit of writing in your journal at the same time every day or week.

I learned how to juggle today!

Experiment with how you write and what you write about. You might prefer to write down whatever pops into your head, or maybe you'd like to build your journal around the same topics every day.

My new guitar!

You could focus on one thing you're hoping to do or achieve, so that you have a record of your progress. This could be learning a new skill, or saving money for something you really want.

I had fun in the park.

Writing isn't the only way to keep a journal. You could also doodle, sketch, or make a voice journal by recording each entry.

Looking at your old journal entries can help you see how things have changed. You might notice a pattern in the way you feel and react in some situations.

2019

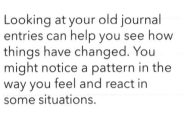

Capturing history

One of the most famous diaries was written by Samuel Pepys in the 1660s. It tells us what life was like at that time, including during the bubonic plague and The Great Fire of London.

Appreciating the good stuff

Making a gratitude journal is a great way to record all the things you're thankful for. Try finishing these sentences, or make up your own.

Today, something that made me smile was...

I am lucky to have these people in my life...

I felt I achieved something when I...

Three good things about today were...

How would you feel?

These people are all having a tough time. How do you think you might you feel in these situations, and how would you act?

Family worries

A family member is in the hospital. They are sad, but visitors cheer them up. How would you feel about visiting them every day? Would it be difficult to stay positive?

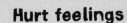

Hurt feelings

Someone at school has said something mean to you. Would you feel angry or upset? How could your friends help?

Left out

Everybody is going to a birthday party except one person. How would you feel if it was you? Would you ask why, or keep quiet?

Understanding others

It's important to try to understand others, but sometimes it's difficult to figure out how someone is feeling and why. Try to put yourself in their situation, then you might be in a better position to help.

People handle things in different ways. How might someone else react in these situations? What could you do to help them?

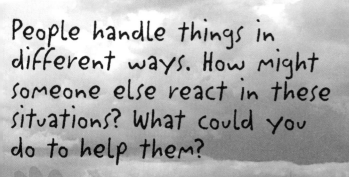

Empathy

Being sensitive to another person's feelings or thoughts is called empathy. It helps you understand people who may be very different from you, or in difficult circumstances. Empathy leads to a world with more kindness.

Future fears

Some people start school halfway through the year. They don't know anyone and everyone has already made friends. Would you feel shy and nervous? What would make it better?

Out of pocket

Imagine all your friends had the latest game console, but you couldn't afford it. Would you feel left out? Could you get excited about saving money to buy it?

Ouch!

Accidents happen. If you break your arm, you might need a cast while it heals. Even simple things such as tying shoelaces can be difficult. Would you feel comfortable asking for help, or would you struggle on by yourself?

Domino effect

The way we act can have a domino effect. This is when one small thing sets off a chain of other things. Different behaviors can cause different domino effects, and they can be positive or negative.

It's all falling down

Imagine someone is really angry about something, and they're in a bad mood. When someone else asks them what's wrong, they yell back meanly. The domino effect might be that they get into trouble for yelling, and their problem doesn't get solved.

I'm still standing

Now, imagine the same person handled the situation differently. Maybe they explained why they were feeling angry and asked for some help. The domino effect could be that they get advice, which makes them feel better.

Someone drops some litter on the street.

Another person copies and drops their litter.

Soon, there is lots of litter in the street.

Ripple effect

Some impacts get bigger and bigger. Littering is one negative example, but on the other hand a single good deed can inspire others to do the same, which then inspires more and more people to be kind.

A seedling of an idea

In 2009, Katie Stagliano brought a cabbage seedling home. She planted it and it grew into a giant cabbage! Katie donated the cabbage to help feed the hungry. Then she started Katie's Krops, which grows crops to feed those in need. This has inspired a lot of people to grow crops for a good cause.

Remember that your actions can affect not only yourself, but other people, too.

Stepping into character

Books and movies have the power to bring characters to life. What do you love about your favorite fictional characters? Try creating your own.

Leaping from the page

Sometimes book characters are so believable you think they could be real. The author may have even based them on someone they know. Can you think of a really interesting character from a book that you love? What is it that makes the character interesting?

From page to screen

Great book characters are often brought to life on screen. Have any of your favorite books been made into a movie or TV series? Do the main characters behave like you imagined them from the book?

"Children often ask me how I invent the characters in my books. It's really just like making up an imaginary friend...".

Jacqueline Wilson

Create a character

Now try inventing your own character! Try to make them different from yourself—think about the way they might behave and why. Start by writing a description of them. Where do they come from? What are their likes and dislikes?

Lights, camera, action...

Finally, imagine you're going to be acting the part of your character on screen. Think about the different situations they could find themselves in. How would they feel? How might they react?

Coping

Going through tough times is part of life. While stressful situations are often hard to avoid, you can learn ways to deal with them and tackle strong feelings, such as anxiety, sadness, and anger.

Keeping your body healthy and your mind calm is a great place to start. Often the most valuable thing you can do to cope with something hard, is to find someone to talk to so you can get the support you need.

skills

Failing to succeed

It can be really frustrating when you don't succeed. It's important, however, that you don't let failure stop you from trying again. Sometimes failing at something can lead to learning, and an even better result.

Try not to get stuck

There will be times when you don't do as well as you had hoped, such as on a school test. It might be hard to accept, but try to move past it. You can't change the past, only the future.

Take on challenges

People who are used to doing well may be worried that they might not be good at something new. This could mean missing out on all kinds of exciting opportunities. Never let the fear of failure hold you back.

Don't give up easily

There may be things in life that you find easy and others that you have to work harder at. It is easy to just give up, but learning to do something that challenges you can be really rewarding.

The best feeling

When you face tricky times, and things don't work out as you planned, you appreciate success more. Celebrating your achievements after a difficult journey is a fantastic feeling!

The right path for you

Failing can make you more determined to succeed at something. It can also open up another path for you to try. You never know, the new path might lead you to a better destination.

Failing has its own rewards

Being able to keep going after failing is a great skill to have. It teaches you valuable lessons and gives you confidence to face the next hurdle, whatever the outcome.

Famous faces who failed first

Some of the world's most successful people have overcome failures in their lives.

Michael Jordan

Basketball star Michael Jordan wasn't picked for his school's top basketball team. He was upset, but this pushed him to work harder for what he wanted.

Oprah Winfrey

Now a world-famous name with her own TV channel, Oprah Winfrey was fired from her first television job. She didn't let failure stand in her way.

Stressful situations

Everyone has times when they feel stressed or anxious. Recognizing how you react to stressful situations is the first step in learning how to manage things better.

Have you experienced any of these common causes of stress and anxiety? How do stressful situations affect you?

Family and home

Sickness in the family

Money problems

Arguing with **parents** or siblings

Not talking to a family member

Moving to a new home

School

Starting a new school

Being teased or bullied

Too much work

Getting into trouble

Feeling like you don't fit in

Fight, flight, or freeze

When your body thinks it's in danger, it can set off an alarm inside that's known as the **fight, flight, or freeze** response. This is your body's way of trying to keep you safe.

What can cause it?

The fight, flight, or freeze response is caused by a release of hormones (chemical messengers in the body) that give you a quick burst of energy. It's usually triggered by emergencies, when there is an immediate threat, but it can also happen in other stressful situations.

What effects does it have?

You might start to breathe faster than usual, which may make you feel light-headed.

The pupils in your eyes may get bigger, so you can spot danger.

You may feel like you need to go to the bathroom.

You may get beads of sweat on your forehead, or sweaty palms.

Your muscles may tense up to prepare you to spring into action.

Your heart beats faster, to pump more blood to your muscles.

Scary headlines

Feeling helpless

Hearing about the suffering of others

World issues

Big issues in the world

Friends moving away

Feeling excluded

Changing friend groups

Arguing with friends

Friends

Caught in a storm

When you have powerful feelings, such as sadness or anxiety, it can feel like you're in the middle of a storm. These emotions can affect you in many ways.

Long-term effects

Most emotions have a short-term effect on your body, such as blushing when you're embarrassed. When emotions become overwhelming, however, they can have a longer-lasting impact. Here are some of the signs to look out for.

Low confidence

If you're struggling with strong feelings, you might start to doubt yourself. This might mean that you don't want to try new things, and you may shy away from seeing your friends.

Avoiding things

Taking part in activities you used to enjoy may feel like a struggle. You may start to make excuses to avoid doing them.

Feeling sick

When your mind is overwhelmed it can affect your body. You may have headaches, stomach problems, or aching muscles.

Sleep changes

If something is troubling you, your sleeping pattern may change. You might find it hard to fall asleep, suffer from nightmares, or sleep more than usual.

Mood swings

You may find yourself feeling really grumpy, or you may overreact to small things. Sometimes this may make you want to lash out at someone.

No concentration

Extreme emotions can make it hard to concentrate. You might have trouble doing your schoolwork.

Light at the end of the tunnel

It's important to remember that all storms will pass, and that these emotions are normal. There are a lot of ways you can manage your feelings, too. Check out the rest of this chapter for ideas and advice.

Choose healthy foods

Eating plenty of fruit and vegetables gives you a boost of vitamins, minerals, and fiber. It's important to eat a wide range of food types, including carbohydrates, such as potatoes and rice, and protein, such as eggs, fish, and beans. Drinking a lot of water is also important.

Move your body

Being active has many benefits. It keeps you fit, reduces stress, and helps you sleep better. Whether you're someone who enjoys playing team sports or you prefer doing an activity by yourself, make time to get moving!

Turn screens off

Too much screen time isn't healthy and can mean missing out on other fun activities. Turning your electronics off for at least an hour before bed can lead to a better night's sleep, too.

Get into a routine

Getting into a good routine is really important. Eating regular meals and going to bed at around the same time every night can make a big difference. Sleeping well is important for your body and mind.

27
November

Healthy habits

Here are nine skills that can help your body and mind stay healthy, and keep stress at bay.

Change the things you can

Consider the daily activities you find difficult. Is there anything you could change, or start doing, to make life less stressful?

Take your mind off things

In times of stress, it can really help to distract yourself. You could do a puzzle, bake a cake, or get crafty, for example. Focusing on something else for a while can help give your mind the break it needs.

Be kind to yourself

Try not to beat yourself up about things. Instead, if you are having a hard time, tell yourself some encouraging words, such as, "Everything is going to be OK."

Find ways to boost your mood

Make time for the small things that bring you joy. You could play with your pet, listen to music, or take a bubble bath. Doing something you enjoy every day can improve your mood and make you feel less stressed.

Spend time with loved ones

Connecting with friends and family can help you relax, and take your mind off things. They might be able to share some helpful advice, or just make you laugh—a great form of stress relief!

Feeling calm

There are many different ways to become calm. Both breathing and mindfulness can help you feel at ease, and balance your emotions.

Careful noticing

Breathing exercises can be calming for some people, but they don't have the same effect on everyone. When you begin, carefully notice how changing your breath feels for you. Here are four exercises to try:

Balloon belly

Pretend that you have a balloon inside your belly. Put your hand on your stomach and breathe in for the count of four, feeling your balloon belly. Pause for two seconds, then breathe out for four, feeling the balloon deflate. Pause for two seconds and repeat.

Shoulder rolling

Roll your shoulders up to your ears as you breathe in. Breathe out through your nose while slowly rolling your shoulders backward and down. Keep rolling and relax.

Feather flutter

Hold a feather in front of your mouth and watch it flutter as you gently blow out. Keeping your attention on the feather can help your worries melt away. You can also put the feather on a flat surface and watch it fly away as you blow.

Nostril breathing

Gently press the side of your nose with one finger, so air only flows through the other side. Breathe in, covering one side, then switch and breathe out while closing the other. Try doing this for three or four breaths.

Focusing on the present

Paying attention to the present moment is called mindfulness. It can help you to stop lingering on past problems and can also stop your thoughts from racing ahead to future worries. Here are four ways to practice mindfulness:

Using your senses

Think about your senses when you take a walk in nature. Notice everything you can see, hear, smell, and touch. What colors can you see? What do the flowers smell like? How does the ground feel under your feet?

Breathing awareness

Being aware of your breathing can be as simple as just closing your eyes and focusing on your breath going in and out. Whenever your mind wanders, try to gently bring your attention back to your breath.

Mindful eating

Before you eat something, try to notice how it feels and smells. Then close your eyes and put the food on your tongue. What is the taste and texture? Now, chew the food very slowly. How does the taste and texture change?

Body scan

Lie down on your back, close your eyes, and let your arms and legs fall out to your side. Breathe in and out deeply, while you focus on each part of your body, moving slowly from the tip of your toes to your head. Notice how each part of your body feels and try to let go of any worries you have.

Seeking support

To get through tough times, one of the best things you can do is to talk to someone about what's happening and how you're feeling.

The problem

Some kids in my class have started picking on me. They are calling me names and pushing me around. I don't want to tell my family because I am embarrassed. I don't know what to do or how to make them stop. What should I do? Who should I talk to?

Asking for help

Talking things out with an adult you trust can often be the best place to start. It could be a parent, grandparent, teacher, or family friend. Sharing your problems can make them feel easier to manage. The person you tell may be able to offer you advice, or find out more about how you can get the help you need.

Starting a difficult conversation

It's not always easy to talk about things that are worrying you. Saying something like, "I'd really like some advice, but I don't know where to start" can help open up the conversation. If you find it too difficult to talk about your problem, you could always write a note.

I am finding it hard to climb to the top, please could I have some help?

Shared experiences

It can really help to talk to someone who has been through a similar experience. People don't always react to things in the same way, but someone who has an understanding of your situation may be able to reassure you that things will get better.

Counseling

There may be times when the best person to help you is a trained counselor or therapist. First, you should talk to a trusted adult so that they can help find the right one for you. Counseling can also be arranged through your doctor or school. The sessions can be face-to-face, over the phone, or online.

Organizations offering support

There are many organizations that offer support to young people for free. Some give advice on a lot of issues, while others focus on something specific, such as mental health, family issues, or bullying. If you need help finding the right organization to help you, ask your school or a trusted adult for advice.

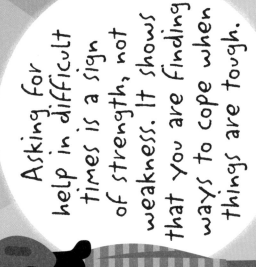

Asking for help in difficult times is a sign of strength, not weakness. It shows that you are finding ways to cope when things are tough.

Don't be scared. I am here to help and to make sure you don't fall.

Plugging into music

Music can reflect almost any emotion. It can make us feel relaxed, energetic, happy, or sad. Singers often write songs to explore things that have happened in their lives.

Lady Gaga

Lady Gaga has written many songs that reflect her life experiences. "Born this Way" is all about learning to love yourself as you are.

Shawn Mendes

In the song "In My Blood," this singer opened up about his feelings of anxiety for the first time.

Something to relate to

Connecting with a book, movie, or song can help you reflect on how you're feeling and realize that others have been through the same thing.

Rihanna

In "Dem Haters," Rihanna sings about her experience of being bullied as a child growing up in Barbados. The lyrics express how the bullying made Rihanna feel.

Ed Sheeran

The song "Afire Love" is about Ed's memories of his grandfather. The lyrics describe how a disease caused Ed's grandfather to lose his memory, and even forget what Ed looked like.

The power of reading

Reading a good book can help to reduce stress, but you can also sometimes find yourself in a book! Reading about a character who is going through similar experiences can help you understand yourself.

Relating to a movie

Movies often tackle difficult topics and can make them easier to understand. If you relate to a fictional character, watching their story unfold on screen can have a big impact on you.

Flying high

Your life skills will continue to develop as you encounter different situations. You don't have to get everything right the first time—the important thing is to learn from each experience and remember to ask for help when you need it. With the right tools on hand, you can look forward to an incredible journey ahead, whatever that may bring.

Help, advice, and information

If you need more information or support, here's a handy list of organizations and websites that could help.

Breathe, Think, Do With Sesame

Bilingual (English and Spanish) app helping children learn Sesame Street's "Breathe, Think, Do" strategy for problem-solving. Teaches skills such as self-control, planning, and task persistence.

Cosmic Kids

Teaches children how to become calm and relaxed through yoga and mindfulness videos.

FunBrain

Created for children in grades pre-K through 8. Offers free interactive games, books, videos, and printables that help develop skills in math, reading, problem-solving, and literacy.

GoNoodle

Teaches movement and mindfulness with free videos created by child development experts.

Headspace for Kids

Teaches children the basics of mindfulness. Kids can practice breathing exercises, visualizations, and try some focus-based meditation. For three age groups: 5 and under, 6–8, and 9–12.

HealthyChildren.org

American Academy of Pediatrics' website containing a wide range of articles and information on children and family health.

Katie's Krops

Encourages children to grow their own crops and donate the harvest to the hungry.

Kidscape

Provides children and adults with advice about how to deal with and prevent bullying.

KidsHealth From Nemours

Provides children and their families information on healthy minds, bodies, and lives.

Kids Help Phone

Kids Help Phone's e-mental health services are available 24/7 for people across Canada.

Awareness days

Empathy Day
June 9th

World Kindness Day
November 13th

World Mental Health Day
October 10th

Kindness UK

Makes kindness a bigger part of daily life, and increase awareness of the benefits of kindness on health and well-being.

Mindfulness4youth

Encourages mindfulness by teaching young people the skills they need to live happier lives.

Minds Matter

Helps high-school students from low-income families by broadening their dreams, and preparing them for college success.

Nourish Interactive

Provides games, tools, and tips on how to live and eat healthily.

PBS Kids

Provides educational games that teach young people to make healthier decisions and live a healthy lifestyle.

Smiling Mind

Provides a web and app-based meditation program to help young people develop the skills they need in life.

STOMP Out Bullying

Works to reduce and prevent bullying by teaching children solutions on how to respond to bullying. Raises awareness and educates children, parents, and teachers about the issue.

Stop, Breathe & Think

An app teaching children to check in on how they are feeling, and encourages calmness.

StopBullying.gov

A federal website that provides information and advice to anyone affected by bullying.

World Health Organization (WHO)

The WHO is part of the United Nations that is responsible for international public health. It identifies the life skills that help children deal with the demands and challenges of daily life.

Glossary

appeal
Attempt to raise money for a good cause

body language
Expressing your feelings and emotions through the way you move and position your body

brainstorm
Thinking up lots of different ways to solve a problem

bullying
Behavior intended to hurt someone physically or emotionally. It may be aimed at a person due to their race, religion, background, disability, or other difference

capture
Being able to express a specific quality, feeling, or part of your personality

charity
Organization that collects money and uses it to help people

con
Negative outcome from doing something, such as making a decision

conclusion
Deciding that something is right or wrong after thinking critically about it

confidence
Feeling sure about your ability to do something

develop
Becoming better or stronger. As you learn and practice the life skills in this book, they will develop

domino effect
When one small thing sets off a chain of other things

emotions
Feelings you have about something, such as happiness when a good thing happens

empathy
Understanding, being aware of, or being sensitive to the feelings, thoughts, and experience of others

emphasize
Drawing attention to

failure
Unsuccessful outcome from doing something

fictional
Something that is made up

fight, flight, or freeze
Internal response everyone has to danger. It's caused by a release of chemical messengers in the body and you'll either face the danger, flee from it, or freeze to protect yourself

flexible
Being open to change and doing something in a different way

fundraising
Raising money for a good cause

habit
Something you do regularly

impact
Effect that something has on a specific situation. For example, the impact of being kind to others is that you make them feel appreciated

intuition
Strong feeling you have about something without thinking too hard about it

kinesics
Study of nonverbal communication

mindfulness
Being aware of yourself in body and mind, and paying attention to the present moment

open-ended questions
Questions where the answer is not just "yes," or "no." These types of question make you think hard about the answer

opinion
View someone has about something

organization
Group of people who work to achieve a common goal

outcome
End result of doing something

personality
What makes you, you! Your personality is your character and the way you act

pro
Positive outcome from doing something, such as making a decision

research
Process by which you gather information to form a carefully considered view about something

stress
Feeling of worry and tension

subconscious
Area of your mind that can influence you without you being aware of it

tone
Way you say something, including the speed, attitude, and emotion you say it with

unique
Special, one-of-a-kind, or unusual

volume
How loud something is, such as your voice when you speak

Index

Acknowledgments

The author would like to thank Nick, Amelie, and baby Elodie, who timed her arrival perfectly for after the book was completed! **DK** would like to thank Helen Peters for the index; Polly Goodman for proofreading; and Jim Green for design assistance.

Quote attribution and references:
pp. 52–53 Barack Obama: "Don't be afraid to ask for help when you need it. I do that everyday. Asking for help isn't a sign of weakness, it's a sign of strength. It shows you have the courage to admit when you don't know something, and to learn something new." From his 2009 speech to students at Wakefield High School, Virginia, US. **pp. 70-71** Jacqueline Wilson: "Children often ask me how I invent the characters in my books. It's really just like making up an imaginary friend…" From a 2017 interview with Penguin Books.

The publisher would like to thank the following for their kind permission to reproduce their photographs:

(Key: a-above; b-below/bottom; c-center; f-far; l-left; r-right; t-top)

6-7 Dreamstime.com: Nadianb. **8-9 Dreamstime. com:** Werner Stoffberg. **10-11 Dreamstime.com:** Hai Huy Ton That / Huytonthat. **12-13 Dreamstime. com:** Photosoup / Hywit Dimyadi. **12 Dreamstime. com:** Jiri Hera (br). **13 Dreamstime.com:** Nataliia Yankovets (cr). **22 Dreamstime.com:** Stocksolutions (bc). **23 Dreamstime.com:** Eric Isselee (ca). **24-25 Dreamstime.com:** Androlia. **28 Dreamstime. com:** Liligraphie (bc); Orcearo / Orcea David (br). **28-29 Dreamstime.com:** Max421. **30 123RF.com:** Maksym Bondarchuk (bl). **30-31 Dreamstime.com:** Maximiliane Wagner. **31 123RF.com:** Maksym Bondarchuk (br). **32 Dreamstime.com:** Mcherevan (clb). **Getty Images:** Moment Open / Paula Sierra (cr). **33 Alamy Stock Photo:** Aflo Co. Ltd. / Nippon News (tr). **Dreamstime.com:** Oleksandra Naumenko (c). **NASA:** (bl). **34-35 Dreamstime.com:** Max421 (t). **38 123RF.com:** Aleksey Boldin (cr). **Alamy Stock Photo:** PG Pictures (tr, br). **40-41 Dreamstime.com:** Kimji10. **45 Dreamstime.com:** Deanpictures (cra). **46 Alamy Stock Photo:** World History Archive (br). **48-49 Dreamstime.com:** Kenneth Ng. **51 Alamy Stock Photo:** Nando Machado (cra).

53 Alamy Stock Photo: DOD Photo (cr). **54-55 Alamy Stock Photo:** B Christopher. **56-57 Dreamstime.com:** Esolex. **59 Getty Images / iStock:** borchee (ca). **60-61 123RF.com:** artenex. **63 Dreamstime.com:** Weedezign (tr). **64 Fotolia:** efired (br). **65 Alamy Stock Photo:** Universal Art Archive (tr). **66-67 Getty Images / iStock:** Olivier DJIANN. **68-69 Dreamstime.com:** Akm Studio. **69 Katie's Krops:** Stacy Stagliano (c). **70-71 Alamy Stock Photo:** Lyle Mallen. **71 Alamy Stock Photo:** WENN Rights Ltd (ca). **72-73 Alamy Stock Photo:** Valentyn Volkov. **75 Alamy Stock Photo:** Geisler-Fotopress GmbH (bc); Rich Kane Photography (crb); maximimages.com (br). **76 Getty Images / iStock:** rogerashford (tr). **77 123RF.com:** pockygallery (crb). **78-79 Dreamstime.com:** Mishoo. **80 Alamy Stock Photo:** PG Pictures (cra). **82-83 Dreamstime.com:** Dmitry Naumov. **86 Alamy Stock Photo:** Bob Daemmrich (tc). **Shutterstock.com:** Tom Rose (cla). **87 Alamy Stock Photo:** Rich Gold (tc); Geoffrey Robinson (cr). **92-93 Dreamstime.com:** Maximiliane Wagner

All other images © Dorling Kindersley
For further information see: www.dkimages.com